Unruly:
The Honest & Rulebook-free Guide
to Modern Wedding Planning

or

How to Plan a Wedding
(and Not Kill Anyone in the Process)

HOLLY POULTER & SUSANNAH DALE

Copyright © 2021 Revelry Events

ISBN: 9798518267268

CONTENTS

INTRODUCTION

We're just going to come out and say it: wedding planning is hard. Organising the best day of your life can be stressful, draining (on you and your wallet) and, let's face it, a right pain in the arse.

Off the back of a year where weddings were postponed or cancelled, reduced and reimagined (thanks, global pandemic), we know that now – more than ever – couples are keen to plan a wedding their way because the doing-things-for-the-sake-of-doing-things argument just doesn't work anymore.

Maybe you're right at the start and trying to figure out what the fuck to do first. Maybe you're in the middle of planning and stressed as hell. Or you just want to avoid killing anyone over chair covers, colour schemes or catering choices. This book is here to help you.

In *Unruly*, you'll find honest advice, budget tips, planning hacks and cheat sheets. What you won't find is bullshit. As planners, we've seen it all – and we're not here to confetti over the cracks.

In each section you'll find references to our handy, fully editable templates to streamline your planning with pre-organised spreadsheets and checklists, which you can find at jointherevelry.com/unrulybook (password at the back, sneaky previewers), while you digest the glorious information in this book. There's also plenty of margin space in here for nerdy annotations and reminders - you're welcome.

It's a stressful time and you don't need clichés or coddling. You want honest, helpful advice from wedding pros who know what it's really like. We hope you find that here.

Let's plan this marriage launch party!

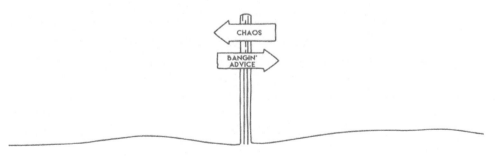

YOU'RE ENGAGED! NOW WHAT THE HELL DO YOU DO?

You're engaged! High five!

Whether it was a total surprise on a romantic weekend in Paris or a 'Hey, you wanna?' at the breakfast table, guess what? You're planning a wedding.

So how do you, like, start doing that?

Step #1: Communicate

I mean, let's *hope* now is not the time you find out your partner has been secretly dreaming of a biker wedding while you've been lusting after a rustic barn do, but we suggest you talk about it just in case.

You might have different ideas on the size, style and location of the wedding day, so it's time to put all your cards on the table. Not unlike a magician. While you're at it you should probably also lay out your position on magicians.

You want to make sure your ideas are in sync right from the start. And if they aren't? Find room for compromise.

Discuss what the most important aspects of the wedding day are to you both – perhaps it's food, headcount, location or music. If you know where your priorities are it will really help you figure out how to put together your budget.

Step #2: Cash money

No one enjoys talking about money, but you need to grit your teeth and agree on a number to avoid running out of it or getting into debt.

How much have you got put aside, how much can you save, and who else might be able to contribute? Knowing how much you are working with will help you set your priorities for spending.

Step #3: Get out the calendar

How long do you need to be able to plan your big day? Do you fancy a mid-summer soiree or a winter celebration?

Consider whether your big day has to be on a weekend at all. Mid-week weddings are increasingly popular, especially after 2020 when everybody postponed to the following season or even further out. Non-weekend weddings will *usually* be kinder on the budget when it comes to venue hire.

Before you book a venue make sure you check with your most important friends and family members that they are available. Let them know your possible wedding date before signing on the dotted line.

Step #4: List the people you don't hate

Draft your wedding guest list but start with *everyone* you can think of. Don't worry about money or venue capacity right now— it's just a useful process. Play a game of Look How Many People I Know.

Then, label your must-haves as your A-list, your would-like-to-haves as your B-list, and your not-the-end-of-the-world-if-they-aren't-there as your C-list.

It might seem a bit brutal doing it this way, but it will give you more flexibility when it comes to venue hunting just in case you fall for a place that changes the headcount you imagined.

Step #5: Get inspired

Well done if you actually waited until step five, but *now* is the time to start getting some ideas from blogs, magazines, Instagram and Pinterest. They are your best friends. But also your enemy. Pinterest is your frenemy. More on that later.

For now, flip and scroll to your heart's content to get a good idea of the style and design of your wedding. Figure out what you do and don't like. Find a cohesive theme, colour scheme or just 'vibe'. Keep all this accessible so you can show your suppliers later.

PLANNING 101:
THE WHAT & THE WHEN

Your timeline is basically going to come down to when you fancy tying the knot. The average length of engagement is now 20 months in the UK (way up from previous years). But that's not to say you *can't* pull together a wedding in a week, we're just saying that week won't be a wedding cakewalk.

For an overview of what you can expect to be doing over the next year or so, follow our *Game of Life*-style to do list, then see our detailed list in the downloads on our website for the proper stuff.

Nice rock! Party time.
↓

How much money are you going to spend though?
Set your budget.

Oh no!
Your parents are giving you some money for the wedding but they want to invite two dozen friends and neighbours. Roll a six to cut that number in half!

12 - 18 MONTHS TO GO

Who do you actually want to be there? Draft your guest list.

↓

Pick a date or time of year to do this thing.

↓

Cool venues! Pick one.

↓

Pick your date with the registrar
if it's a legal sitch.

↓

Snap! Find photographers and videographers you like.

↓

Yum! Look into potential caterers.

↓

What are you going to wear? Start the sartorial hunt!

↓

Bummer! You slept in and missed the sample sale.
Skip a go!

8 - 10 MONTHS TO GO

Send out those save-the-dates.

↓

Stop and smell the roses. Book your florist!

↓

Book your music and entertainment.

↓

6 MONTHS TO GO

Order your wedding cake.

↓

Get dolled up and have a
hair-and-makeup trial.

↓

Look into transport for you and your guests.

↓

Order or hire all your decor and furniture.

↓

Buy your accessories and order the suits.

3 - 4 MONTHS TO GO

Timing is everything! Draft your schedule.

↓

Send out your proper invites.

↓

Order those wedding rings.

↓

Oh no! Your bestie from uni can't make it.
Skip a turn while you have a little cry.

↓

Stat working on that ceremony plan.

↓

Order all your on-the-day stationery.

6-8 WEEKS TO GO

Final dress fittings. You look amazing!
Take a bonus card.

↓

Chase those pesky missing RSVPS.

↓

Tell everyone what they are supposed to be doing
and when.

4-6 WEEKS TO GO

Sweet! Everything paid up on time.
Have another free turn!

↓

Share all the final details with your
suppliers and key people.

↓

Put your playlists together.

1 WEEK TO GO

Pack for wedding-day kit.

↓

Make final arrangements for honeymoon!

↓

Oh dear cousin Margot forgot to tell you she's GF and vegan now. Skip a go while you figure out with the caterer what the hell she can eat.

THE DAY BEFORE

Hold rehearsal if you want/need one.

↓

Get your last minute decor finished

↓

Get some sleep - zzzzz.

D-DAY

Marry the shit out of each other!

THE 7 EMOTIONAL STAGES OF WEDDING PLANNING

Planning a wedding means emotions are going to be in hyperdrive for months. There are times when you are on actual cloud nine, and others where you want to crawl under the duvet and never utter the words 'table plan' ever again.

It's. Totally. Normal.

If you're right at the start, somewhere in the middle, or out the other side we're sure some of these stages will strike a chord.

Euphoric

What You Say: "I mean it was honestly such a surprise, I had no idea!"

What You Mean: "I have been practising my 'shocked but still cute' face for months in case he ended up having this proposal secretly filmed"

What You Should Do: WhatsApp everyone you know with a coy and clever announcement while simultaneously signing up for every wedding blog newsletter you can find. But most importantly, celebrate! Make the most of this euphoria and really drag out the champagne period.

Manic

What You Say: "Babe, I've scheduled three venue visits for this Saturday morning, then we're going to meet with the photographer to chat about our engagement photos. Sunday I was thinking we should go browse for gift-list items? Then my mum is staying with us for a week to help me pick out a dress. Cool?"

What You Mean: "I'm drowning in wedmin and I don't know what I'm supposed to be doing first. Therefore, I'll just do everything at once. Yes, that's a good plan."

What You Should Do: Relax, write down everything you're trying to do and put it in priority order. Don't put pressure on yourself to sort everything out in the first few months. Make time for enjoying the engagement and each other.

Fatigued

What You Say: "I literally can't look at another swatch of table cloths. They are all the same. It's the worst kind of Fifty Shades of Grey."

What You Mean: "I've taken on too much too soon and I am wedding-ed out. If another person asks me how planning is going I might smack them."

What You Should Do: Delegate. Either to family and friends or a professional. Get rid of some of the boring tasks, the ones that you're getting nowhere on or are doing your head in. You also need to take a wedding break at this point, step away from the spreadsheet. It can be really freakin' draining to plan the best day of your life, so do something else and come back to it.

Anxious

What You Say: "That's okay, Aunt Karen, no worries. Sure, we can wait a few more weeks to get your 100% confirmed RSVP. Oh you might be bringing a date? Grreeeeeat."

What You Mean: "Fuck you, Karen it's £150 per head. PER HEAD!"

What You Should Do: It can be super frustrating when people aren't playing ball and adhering to *your* timeline. A lot of people who haven't been through planning a wedding genuinely have no idea how much this can stress you out. And even those who have been through it can conveniently forget. Be calm and give people earlier deadlines so you avoid chasing and giving yourself anxiety.

Frenzied

What You Say: "I know it's 1 am, Mum, but I need to make sure the venue has this list of the 40 DIY'd things I have left in the boxes so they know precisely where to put them tomorrow. I'll just be another 3-7 hours. Max."

What You Mean: "I am freaking out about getting married and everything going wrong for this day that I poured my heart, soul and piggy bank into"

What You Should Do: Seems too easy to say it, but you really do need to relax. If you have followed our sage advice, you know that you will have done everything you can do at this stage.

But honestly? Something *will* go wrong. It probably won't be big, you probably won't even notice it, but it's a safe bet that something will go slightly off-piste. Maybe the dinner will run 15 minutes over, or someone's mic doesn't work on the first go, or your flower girl turns and runs the other way at the top of the aisle (classic). But remember, these are the things that will make for good stories after the wedding. Don't hold your perfect plans so tightly that the slightest hiccup will sour your mood for the rest of the day. Shrug it off and hit the dance floor. The important thing is that you're marrying the (hopefully) love of your life.

Relieved (and happy)

What You Say: "Oh, wasn't it such a great day, I wish I could do it all over again."

What You Mean: "Holy shit, we did it! All our time and energy and money was actually worth it! #smugmarrieds!"

What You Should Do: Absolutely fucking nothing. Bask in the glorious feeling of not having to wade through spreadsheets, papercut your tongue licking envelopes or worry about not fitting into your dress (hello, hotel breakfast in bed).

Eventually you should get round to writing your gift list thank-yous and emailing your suppliers, check your Facebook photo tags (approve, approve, delete) and enjoy some well-deserved time off.

Melancholy

What You Say: "Wow, what an amazing honeymoon! Well, here comes Monday."

What You Mean: "My life has no meaning anymore. No offence, babe."

What You Should Do: The post-wedding blues are real and it sucks. You've spent months, maybe years, planning your wedding and now it's done. The planning of a single day no longer occupies the majority of your brain.

Plan something else. Something big (if you have any money left), like a birthday or your next holiday. Or even something super small, like your next date night or weekend brunch plans. Sometimes even sending a thoughtful, impromptu gift or greetings card to a friend will help you shift the focus onto someone else and get you some endorphins back.

IT'S NOT ABOUT THE MONEY, MONEY, MONEY (EXCEPT IT KIND OF IS THOUGH)

We'll level with you. Wedding budgets are hard. You feel like you need an economics degree to work out how to set and stick to a budget.

In truth, there is no typical amount you're meant to spend on anything; all venue and supplier costs vary depending on location, style and quality. And contrary to popular belief, suppliers *don't* stick another zero on the end when you say the word wedding. Maybe they did once upon a time but it's a competitive market now and most suppliers are small businesses or one-man bands who are just trying to do a good job, especially after an enormously shit year for the wedding industry.

There are so many variables with a budget. We can't wave a magic wand and tell you exactly how much everything will cost (sorry), but we *can* offer some advice to make it a bit easier for you. And, of course, we have a budget tool in the master template which you can use to set and manage your own budget.

So what's the first thing you should know? Half of your budget will be used up by costs relating to your venue, food and drink. Yep, we know, that sounds like a lot, and no, it's not an exact science because every wedding is different, but it's a good starting point. If the cost of your venue and catering look like it's going wildly over that halfway line you've perhaps picked a venue that's too expensive, in which case it's time to think about increasing the wedding pot.

The next thing you should know is how to approach your budget and with this we have just one word – **PRIORITIES**. If there's one thing we could drum into your head it would be to know your priorities and put them at the very top of your budget list. If something is important to you, that's where you want to spend your cash.

Finally, look for *value for money*, not *saving money* - there is a difference. For example, you can pick up a pair of high street shoes that work perfectly with your dress for £25. You're only going to wear them once - what's the point in paying more, right? But what if that one time wear is for ten hours, how comfortable are those shoes going to be when you want to hit the dance floor at 11 pm? Buy a better pair and your feet will thank you.

It works the other way too. You can serve Champagne during a drinks reception but most people can't tell the difference between that and Prosecco – some even prefer the latter. Choose the cheaper option; most guests will be none the wiser, even less of them will care.

PUTTING A RING ON IT: THE LEGAL (& NOT SO LEGAL) OPTIONS

Getting married is a contract, which means there are rules, a whole lot of rules. If you want to make your love legal you need to abide by them with a straight face.

Legal weddings are either religious or civil – they cannot be both. Church and state and all that. If you have a religious wedding it's in a place of worship. A civil wedding is in a licensed structure (England and Wales only, Scotland is more flexible) and can't include any religious readings or songs.

In this chapter we're going to give you a step-by-step guide to getting married the legal way, plus some not-so-legal advice (but not the kind we could get sued for). Just to be clear, this chapter is about civil ceremonies only – if you're planning to have a religious wedding it's best to speak directly to your regular place of worship.

1. For a civil ceremony, start by picking your licensed venue and booking your date.

2. Once you have your date and venue, you can call the registry office local to the venue where you're going to get married. The government website has a handy tool to help you find the right one, you just need to enter the postcode of the venue. Tell them your venue and date and they will book a registrar for you. You normally get a choice of times, but try to contact as early as you can – the registrar's availability dictates the time of your service. Registrar prices vary per location.

3. Give notice at your local registry office up to 12 months before your wedding. Giving notice is a process where you and your partner go to your registry office together (local to where you live, not your wedding venue) and tell them your intent to marry. You must do this at least 28 days before your wedding day. This is normally £35 per person.

4. At your appointment you both need to take proof of your name, age and nationality such as a passport, and proof of address such as a driving license or bill.

5. During the appointment they'll speak to you both together and individually to get your information and ensure that you and your partner know each other as a genuine couple. After this they will display your intent to marry for 28 days.

6. Your registrar will probably call you a couple of days before your wedding to go over the details of the day with you.

7. On the day you don't need to take any documents or ID with you, but you will need to meet with the registrar separately to re-confirm the details you gave when you first gave your notice. This will need to be done at the venue before the ceremony and only takes five minutes (it's known as an interview).

8. The ceremony itself will only last about ten to fifteen minutes, but you can add in your own readings and songs (as long as they aren't religious, offensive or deafeningly loud) to make it worth turning up for.

9. You'll need to nominate two people over the age of 16 to act as your witnesses; they will also sign the register during the ceremony.

10. You'll be handed a marriage certificate at the end of the ceremony. Give it to someone you trust for safekeeping. (Handy hint: order two certificates for your wedding day, it's cheaper than ordering an extra one after the wedding. If you're planning to change your name(s) you'll have to post an original several times so there's always a risk one can get lost).

11. You are now wed and can start drinking.

So that's how you do it legally, easy right? But what if you want an outdoor wedding, you want to include different faiths in one ceremony, or simply just to have a ceremony that is more personalised? You could hire a celebrant and have a blessing.

A celebrant is a trained professional who will conduct your wedding ceremony in the style you want, so you can create a service more personal to you in any location. Even if the venue is licensed you can still use a celebrant. However, this is *not* a legal wedding, and and you will have to do the steps above to bind you together in the eyes of the law at a separate time at your own convenience.

Having a blessing on your wedding day (which most guests don't realise isn't legal anyway) isn't always just down to wanting a more personalised service — sometimes it's about the location.

England and Wales have strict rules on where wedding ceremonies can take place. It has to be in a licensed structure and it's only licensed if it's a permanent structure with a roof. We told you there were rules.

If you've dreamt of a woodland wedding or getting hitched on a beach then you might want to think about getting a celebrant on the day, doing the legal stuff before or after. Or you could go toScotland where — along with the wonders of haggis — they really know what they're doing with weddings (side note, one of us lives in Glasgow, so we're biased).

And just to touch on Scottish weddings, they do still have a legal requirement to give notice – the main difference is that you can pretty much get married anywhere (perfect for elopements or micro-weddings) as long as the person marrying you is approved to do so.

And now back to celebrants – they vary in cost and style so if you decide to go down that route, do your research and meet a couple to make sure the chemistry is right.

A couple of websites to get you started are:

http://www.professionalcelebrants.org.uk/
https://humanism.org.uk/ceremonies/

He Said/She Said: Supplier Edition

Celebrant **Nat Raybould** says, "Take time to choose the celebrant that is truly right for you: they will be representing and celebrating your unique relationship, and so you have to really click with them to be able to trust them with your hearts. Your wedding ceremony should be the glittering highlight of your wedding day!"

VENUES: FINDING SOMEWHERE TO SAY I DO

Finding the ideal backdrop for your nuptials is probably the most intimidating part of wedding planning. Seriously, there are literally thousands of options and things to consider – where do you even start?

That question was, of course, rhetorical because we're going to tell you. You're welcome.

What kind of venues can I have?

Before you start thinking about the tiny details of what your venue needs, it's time for a little back-to-basics overview of the types of wedding venue available to you. We'll cover marquees and tents later.

Of course, this isn't a catch-all guide but it covers the majority of venues we have in old Blighty, and will give you an idea of which way you're leaning.

COUNTRY HOUSES

PROS

✦Fancy as hell

- ✦ Exclusive use of the entire venue, often for more than just the day

- ✦ Lots of different rooms at your disposal

CONS

- ✦ Can be expensive, especially if you're getting the run of the house for the weekend

HOTELS

PROS

- ✦ Built-in accommodation for you and your family and friends

- ✦ Experienced staff already on site to help set up, pack down and everything in between

- ✦ Most furniture already included

CONS

- ✦ Often offer package deals which cover everything from venue hire to the cake knife, which can feel restricting

- ✦ You may have a problem with exclusivity if it's a big hotel with lots of reception rooms, or even just other hotel guests wandering around

+ Specific design (watch out for those carpeted ball-rooms)

OUTDOOR SPACES

PROS

+ Total blank canvas

+ Use any suppliers you want to as you're bringing everything in yourself

+ Natural decor in the surroundings mean you may not have to decorate as much as other places

+ Sometimes cheaper to hire, and usually option of using it for the weekend or longer - so guests can glamp or camp on site

CONS

+ Weather - plan B needed if it's wet or really, really hot

+ Marquees and tents (more on that later) can be expensive once you add everything up like flooring, lighting, catering tents, generators and toilets

+ Rare to find an outdoor space licensed for legal weddings in England and Wales (rules are legal weddings have to be under a fixed structure like an arbor or a gazebo), but not impossible

RESTAURANTS

PROS

✦ Pretty much guaranteed good food and drink

✦ Professional staff

✦ Most furniture already included

CONS

✦ May not be as much space available for dancing

✦ Unlikely to be a legal ceremony venue

WAREHOUSES, URBAN SPACES + STUDIOS

PROS

✦ Modern blank canvas

✦ Huge flexibility in terms of how you want to decorate

✦ Typically in cities, so easy for guests to get to

CONS

✦ Usually dry hire, which means you pay for the venue only – no staff, catering, furniture, heating, anything. So you have to bring all of that in yourself

HISTORICAL VENUES

PROS

+ Glamorous backdrop – the venue speaks for itself when it comes to decor

+ Likely options of indoor and outdoor if it's on an estate

CONS

+ Restrictions on suppliers you can bring in, they will often only allow people they trust

+ Restrictions on other things like heels, red wine, berries (yep) and confetti

Priorities

Now try a fun little experiment. Separately or together, write down up to ten must-haves about your ideal wedding venue. From the broad location to the specific decor choices.

Ask yourselves whether these kind of things are important to you and your search for the perfect venue:

+ What style of venue do we have our hearts set on?

✦ Realistically, how much can we spend on venue and catering?

✦ How many people do I need to fit in this venue? (though you might fall in love with a smaller venue and cull your imaginary guest list accordingly)

✦ Do we want to be surrounded by nature or the city?

✦ Do we like the idea of a chic hotel wedding or a rustic country barn do?

✦ Does it need to be near a certain city? How far are we willing to ask people to travel?

✦ Does it even need to be in the UK?

✦ Do we really mind if it's licensed for legal weddings or would we have two venues?

✦ Do we want to bring in our own caterers?

✦ Do we need a lot of parking? A helipad, even, if we're feeling flashy.

✦ Does it matter if it doesn't have an outdoor space?

✦ Will we need a lot of accommodation nearby?

✦ Do we want somewhere we can spend a weekend or just a one-day celebration?

There are a ton more questions but this should get you into a space where you're prioritising what's really important to you – what you see when you picture you and your other half really getting married.

Swap lists if you worked separately. See what kind of crossover priorities you have and where you both might be willing to compromise to find your true top 5 deal breakers.

Now you've got your brief, it's time to start researching!

Research

So by now you've probably got a good idea of what you're looking for, and where you're looking. Google your heart out and start adding to our venue search tab in the downloadable.

Log all of the venues you like the look of at face value (hello, impressive Instagram feed!) before you delve deeper into seeing if it's right for you.

If you're struggling with where to look and your brain is tired from figuring out key search terms to find what you want, try a few other routes:

✦ Ask friends! Someone's cousin's friend's neighbour got married somewhere you might like. It's definitely worth a go.

- ✦Instagram - follow some wedding suppliers you like the look of to see *where* they are working and if anything strikes you.

- ✦Follow specific geographical tags like #london-wedding or #cotswoldswedding to see if anything new comes up.

- ✦Literally search 'venue' or the type of venue you're looking for in Google maps, it will throw up various spaces that might not be listed in other directories if you're looking in a specific location.

- ✦Council websites will have a comprehensive list of which venues in their area are licensed for civil ceremonies, to save you searching.

- ✦Check directories. Some are a bit of a free-for-all and there is no quality control, but there are a few good venue directories out there that are easy to use with great options.

With your glorious venue spreadsheet in front of you, you should now have a good idea of which ones are ticking the boxes for you,. Get in contact and ask for more information to find out price range and availability. Et voila, you have your shortlist.

From your shortlist of up to ten venues (more than that seems unwieldy), select your frontrunners and arrange some site visits!

Venue visits

Ideally, just the two of you (plus maybe your wedding planner – hi!) would be attending your first viewing of a wedding venue.

The temptation to bring along parents and friends is strong, but just as with outfit appointments, sometimes the first time is better with a smaller group. You want to be able to form your own first impression and not be swayed by the approving or disapproving noises of others. If you like it enough to have a second viewing just to make sure, then you can bring along as many parents and besties as you can fit through the door (don't quote us on that).

Take your time and get your tour through the venue, and if you can save up your questions for after you're done you'll have a clearer understanding of context for them.

So what the devil do you need to know? It's important to cover the details to be sure this is the right venue for you. Now is the time to discover the cons to the venues pros - no venue is perfect. So find out any issues at the start and decide if there are any deal breakers.

Remember, in our downloadable you'll find our list of all important questions you need each venue to answer for you to be able to make your final choice.

It might seem like a lot, but trust us - you'll feel so much better having these answers ahead of time to avoid descending into bridezilla rage months later. Don't feel too overwhelmed by this list. The chances are you already know some of the answers from your research and the venue manager will cover off a lot of it as you tour the venue.

Once you've asked all your questions, ask if you can put the date on hold for a week or two, or have them call you as soon as someone else enquires about the date to give you some breathing space before you make a decision.

Making a booking

Do we have a frontrunner? Are we ready to lay down some cash for this joint? Hooray!

Once you've let your favourite venue know and confirmed the date is still available, they will send you some boring but important pieces of paper to read through before making it official. Make sure you don't miss any hidden costs or restrictions by carefully reading everything through to make sure you're not agreeing to any clauses that might make planning difficult.

✦ Check what is included and not, so you aren't being charged extra for things that you thought were part of the package

+ Look for hidden fees like penalties for late pay-ments, post-event clean up, overtime of staff or damage to property

+ Make sure VAT has been added already, because that could be a nasty surprise

+ Be aware that the deposit will be due when you sign the contract, so make sure you have funds ready to roll

+ Find out when other payments are due. Most commonly, venues ask for some now some after the wedding, others sprinkle instalments through-out the year – so find out which one it is

GETTING FROM A TO B

If you end up booking two venues for ceremony and reception, you'll be aiming to get all your guests from A to B without losing anyone on the way. If you don't have any old tracking devices left over from your KGB days (our lips are sealed), put a helpful wedding party or family member in charge of this, one that won't get too drunk too soon.

Make sure they know how many guests you have and they can do a headcount to make sure everyone is still around – like a school trip, but with alcohol.

Try to avoid venues that are more than 40 minutes apart as that's a long time to be sitting on a bus or in a car, and more opportunity to get lost or stuck in traffic.

However, if you have got venues that have a fair distance between them keep your guests entertained with some games or quizzes to make sure everyone is still chatting and having a good time.

SHELTER ME:
MARQUEES + TENTS

Whether you're throwing your party in a rural field or a country manor estate, it's likely you're going to be booking some kind of marquee, tent or tipi. Lots of couples assume that having a marquee wedding is going to be easy and budget-friendly.

Let us drop some unwelcome truth bombs on this one.

It's not going to be cheaper. And it's *not* usually easier. Unless it's in your own garden or your family have some land you can use – lucky!

Don't get us wrong. Wedding tents can be oh-so-beautiful and they are the perfect opportunity for a blank canvas, to build something from scratch and put your own personality into your day. But that's also the same reason it can be a frickin' huge challenge, which couples shouldn't take lightly.

Here are five things you should take into consideration when you're thinking about holding all or part of your day under canvas.

Style + space

From geo-domes and pagoda marquees to rustic tipis and clearspan 'greenhouse' design, there are so many options to choose from. It all comes down to the style of your day as a whole (as well as your budget). And consider the scenery – how will your structure look against it?

Here are a few examples of some of the main tent styles.

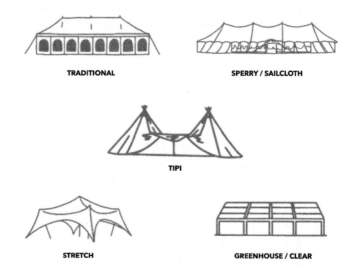

TRADITIONAL

SPERRY / SAILCLOTH

TIPI

STRETCH

GREENHOUSE / CLEAR

Think about the ground you're working with too -- marquees and tents usually need a flat surface (that isn't liable to flood), so make sure you have the marquee company do a site visit before confirming your order.

Call for assistance

In most cases, couples opt for a marquee when they book a dry-hire venue with little or no indoor space, which can mean zero staff. And since you're bringing in everything yourself, it's a good idea to call in the professionals and have someone manage all the bookings, deliveries and schedule on the day – AKA a wedding planner or on-the-day coordinator. A lot of marquee companies also offer staff to be on site; they can assist with rolling the sides up or down, working the generator and so on.

Access

Your tent will normally need up to two days to be erected (stop laughing), so you'll need to check with your venue when you can do that. Assuming you're getting married on a Saturday, most venues will let you set up from Friday, and some will let you in to build from Wednesday or Thursday, with pack-down on the Sunday or Monday.

Some of your other suppliers might need early access too. Your florist and lighting supplier might need to come in the day before to rig anything you're doing with the ceiling, and your caterers will want to set out tables and chairs as early as possible.

For guests walking from the car park, most marquee companies provide matting - you don't want guests slipping in mud before your ceremony, those clumsy fools!

Extra costs

The extra things you can get for a marquee wedding are a bit endless, and all depend on your setup and your preference. But think about:

✦ Flooring (matting or wood)

✦ Lighting, inside and outside (don't underestimate this, no one wants to walk to the toilet or their tent in the dark)

✦ Generators (often sub-contracted by the marquee company and included in the cost but be sure to ask about it)

✦ Catering tents and walkways

✦ Toilets (and showers if you're glamping)

✦ Furniture – some companies offer furniture to match the style of the marquee

It all adds up, so make sure you have budgeted correctly from the start, which you can do with our handy budget tab in the downloadable template.

THE WEDDING PARTY MINEFIELD

Selecting your A-Team can be tricky. With a mix of friendship groups, pushy in-laws and weird family obligations, it's a minefield of emotion (and terror).

Who to ask

Before you get overexcited and WhatsApp your besties, chat about who you think would be the right fit for your wedding party on *both* sides.

Choose people who are supportive, helpful, fun and honest. Friends and family you *know* will get stuck in when they need to. Choose groups you think will get along together, even if they don't know each other yet – wedding party tension is the last thing you want on your big day.

And if you have to make some tough decisions not to include some people who might be expecting you to, remember there are other ways to keep them involved. Good speaker? Let them give a reading at the wedding. Loves to bake? Ask them to whip up something tasty for the favours.

Some fun rules about not having rules...

DON'T ask someone to be in your wedding party <u>just</u> because you were in theirs

DON'T feel like you have ask anyone unless it's literally going to get you in some serious trouble with family and you would be racked with guilt until death

DON'T feel like you need an even number on both sides

DO have a mixed wedding party if you have a mix of genders in your inner circle

DON'T feel obligated to include all the littles of your family or give kids of your friends jobs to do on the day – that shit can get out of control fast

How many?

It can be tempting for indecisive/people-pleaser types to just ask a ton of friends and family and be done with it but that can be overwhelming and costly, especially if you decide to pay for the outfits.

It's also more diaries to sync for fittings, hen and stag weekends and even the big day itself. The average is four on each side of a wedding party, but you can do whatever you feel is right for you (and your wallet).

What am I asking?

Consider what kind of role you want your wedding party to play during your engagement and on your the day. Do you just want cheerleaders, to get you excited and motivated? Do you want doers, who will be on the production line of favour-making and putting their saliva on envelopes? Or is it purely for the optics? Set expectations for your team and consider who out of your friends and family best fits the job description.

So what is it that bridesmaids and groomsmen are meant to do?

Typical bridesmaids' duties

From the get-go the most important duty of a bridesmaid is to be your encourager, your reliable confidant about all things wedding. It's just as much about the emotional needs as it is about the planning. You are, at some point, going to freak the fuck out and need someone to give you a verbal chill pill.

In more practical terms, bridesmaids duties during the planning process can be anything from shopping for the dress to stuffing envelopes – you have to be clear about what you're expecting from each bridesmaid to avoid a lot of unnecessary stress down the line! They can't read your mind so let them know where you're at when you ask them and keep them involved throughout.

Planning the hen night is another major duty for the bridesmaids - they need to plan activities and events which they know you will love without it breaking the bank for everyone that's invited.

The day before they might need to attend the rehearsal and/or help put any last-minute decor together. And on the big day itself - help you get dressed, tell you how great you look, make it all about you, and get you refreshments when you need it. And if you're wearing a big ol' dress, don't forget they may need to help you, an adult, go to the bathroom at some point too.

You may want one or all of your bridesmaids (Lord help you if it's all) to give a toast or a speech. Because, equal rights. Brief them on timings and what you really, really don't want them to mention in front of your new in-laws.

Typical groomsmen jobs

You mean aside from helping to organise the most *legendary* stag do of all time?

Best men, groomsmen and ushers will need to help out the groom with choosing outfits and probably go to get measured for a suit to buy or hire.

Whereas the bridesmaids find themselves busy in the run up and more chilled on the day, most of the groomsmen jobs come about the day before and the day of the wedding, and it might get pretty hands on.

You might need to enlist your ushers and best men to come down to the venue and help with whatever setup you can do beforehand, especially if it's dry hire and you need to set out things like tables, chairs and decorations yourself.

When guests arrive, ushers will direct them to their seats and make sure the front rows are reserved for wedding party and close family. They might hand out the order of service as they come in, and direct people to the facilities.

After the ceremony, bridesmaids and groomsmen will often need to get everyone in place for the all-important confetti shot and other general herding of people.

Make sure these aren't all thankless tasks. Your wedding party commits a lot of time and energy to being there for you, so thank them and, if you can, give them a little something as a token of gratitude.

And of course, all of the above is just traditional expectations. Don't be afraid to mix it up however you want. As long as you've got the jobs covered on the day and you both feel supported then you're golden.

SUPPLIERS: HOW TO FIND YOUR WEDDING DREAM TEAM

Booking all your wedding suppliers can seem like a mammoth task. Finding people you trust with the happiest day of your life? No mean feat.

So here's how you can smash this task with style.

Where to find people

There are a hundred different ways wedding professionals are able to market themselves these days. Wedding fairs, magazines, blogs and social media are a great source of information. But the all-time best place to begin is with word of mouth.

Crowdsource recommendations from friends, family and any suppliers you've already booked. Venues often have a list of suppliers they trust which is a good starting point, but do your own research as well – some venues receive a commission from the suppliers on their list. That's not to say they're not good suppliers, it's just a business arrangement they have with the venue but it's ok to ask your venue how they put together their list, just to be sure you're getting good advice based on previous work and not a wad of cash.

A note on awards, accreditation + cheeky people

Hey, fun fact! The wedding industry – from photographers and planners to bloggers and stationers – is largely unchecked and unregulated. Surprise!

This means there are no laws that govern what happens in the industry and no one officially checking that everyone is qualified, experienced and insured. Anyone can set up a website and start being a wedding pro with the right motivation.

So don't freak out! It just means that couples like yourselves have to do a *little* bit more digging and due diligence to make sure you are putting your trust in the right people.

✦ If they have won awards, how recent are they?

✦ Check testimonials and Google reviews

✦ Check portfolios include images from real weddings rather than just styled shoots. Styled shoots are creative shoots put together by a collaboration of wedding professionals, often for PR purposes. They are great to show off creativity and build contacts with other suppliers, but they cannot replace real wedding experience.

If the portfolio is not labeled into different real-life weddings albums the easiest way to tell you're probably only looking at styled shoots is weddings that don't include a full set up shot of the dining room or a real-looking couple. All wedding professionals have to start somewhere and styled shoots are a great way to do this, but make sure the quote you're given reflects this. It's fair to expect a higher fee from a photographer or planner with 100 weddings under their belt vs 10.

How to choose?

Get quotes from at least three different suppliers to get a sense of cost. As we said in the budget section, there is no one-size-fits-all wedding, but if you get a few quotes you can get a feel for the right price and also manage your expectations.

We strongly advise a video call or meeting with suppliers that you might have a more personal relationship with like a planner or photographer. You need to feel comfortable with this person during planning and on the day itself.

Small print

Once the booking has been confirmed and contract signed give your shortlisted suppliers a courtesy email to let them know you have gone with someone else. Don't feel bad, they will be alright! It's all part of the gig, but if they know you've picked another supplier they can accept another enquiry for your date.

Wait until you've signed on the dotted line though, most suppliers will reserve your date as default and let you know if someone else wants to take it, but in case it slips through the gap and another couple steal your supplier (scandal!) at least you have a shortlisted option to fall back on.

Read all the contracts super carefully, make a note of when instalments are due and if your suppliers have any special requirements.

When everything does go through and you have 100% confirmed with your supplier, here's how not to piss off and be pissed off by your suppliers:

DO keep in touch with your suppliers about anything that might relate to their role on your day, but don't overdo it. If you booked your caterers a year in advance, you don't need to decide the way the napkins will be folded until much, much later. Be aware you aren't their only client between now and your wedding.

DON'T call them out of hours unless you have something scheduled. Yes, we all try to go above and beyond – and since couples usually have nine-to-five jobs, they often only get to wedding tasks out of office hours. But many suppliers work weekends as well as during the day, so their evenings are time for family, friends and binge watching when possible.

DO check the rider. Sometimes suppliers, like bands, have riders which outline what they need to have available on the day. This could be anything from bottled water and snacks to oddly specific beer and rooms of kittens (though probably not unless you can afford Mariah). Check what you're agreeing to so you don't fall into any traps.

DON'T ask suppliers to copy other people's work (to an extent). Pinterest is a brilliant tool for collecting images of wedding details you like, but don't use it as a blueprint for your suppliers to copy *exactly*. Trust in the expertise of the dream team you chose to create something unique for you, using your images as a guideline. You paid a lot of money for this person's skill, so use it and be pleasantly surprised!

TIME TO CULL THE PEOPLE YOU ONLY TOLERATE

Spoiler alert! One of the biggest reasons weddings cost so much is the number of people attending. Get that guest list down and you have less people to feed and water throughout the day. It may sound brutal, but culling people is the best way forward – trust us, it's cathartic. However, that's not always easy to do when you're locked in a tug-of-war with family and friends who want a say in your guest list.

Welcome to our own brand of modern wedding etiquette that will help you navigate these stormy guest list waters.

What to do when your parents want to invite their friends

This is your wedding *but*...did your parents give you any money towards it? If the answer is no, you can move on to the next section with your conscience intact. If you're paying for everything, the guest list is your call.

However, if like most people the Bank of Mum and Dad have helped you out, it's only fair to recognise that. Now we're not saying every Tom, Dick and Sandra deserve an invite, but talk to your parents and agree on a suitable number of people.

To soften the blow of having someone you've barely met at your wedding, remember, you'll probably get a gift out of it...

What to do about your friends' partners who you don't really know, like or have never met

It's all about the evening invite for this one. The time between the invitations going out and the wedding can be a good couple of months so if a friend gets a new partner in that period don't feel obliged to re-arrange your table plan, just extend an invite to the evening do.

However, if you have a friend who has been with their partner for a while and you don't really know them, like them or think they'll last long-term you may have to suck it up to avoid putting anyone's nose out of joint.

The best way to handle a situation like this is be consistent with all guests. Either invite no partners, only married partners, or people that have been together a year or more.

Whatever you chose to do, make it consistent. If you need to have an awkward conversation with a friend, be clear that it's a rule you've made across the board.

What to do about your friends' snot-nosed kids / little angels

What's that? You think kids are the key to any good wedding? Great, enjoy.

For those of you who can't think of anything worse than a crying baby during your vows (do not rely on the parent leaving the room, they will stand at the back and forget that sound *does* travel) or a small child sliding on their knees across the dance floor, this section is for you, pal.

First off, kids in the family. If it's a close family member (like a sibling) and they've got a couple of munchkins, forget it - they're coming. Wave your white flag now and surrender yourself to that inevitability. But here's the trick — give them a role so they feel like they're part of the day. Something like 'guest book protector' or 'dress fluffer-upper'. Even the smallest thing can make some kids feel important and on their best behaviour.

In most other cases it's all about consistency and a little bit of tact. Before the invites go out, speak to guests with kids and let them know the wedding will be child-free (excluding nephews or nieces if you have them). Put it to them this way: you're doing them a favour. It will mean they can have a break and really enjoy themselves (we have four children between us and we *don't* have fun with our kids at weddings). If you're friends with normal people they'll be thrilled.

When it comes to the invites follow through and make it clear who is invited by putting their exact names and not 'The Surnames'. If you need to include a line about kids not being part of the day, do so, but keep it short and sweet.

Now you've read all our advice, go ahead and put your guest list together. Feel free to use our handy guest list tool in our downloadables.

IT'S NOT ABOUT THE SIZE, IT'S HOW YOU PLAN IT: A NOTE ON MICRO-WEDDINGS

Despite 2020 (and most of 2021) being an absolute car-crash in general, it's fair to admit there were a few gems to come out of the chaos, some silver linings of new normal – working from home in your pyjamas on the reg, table service even in fast food restaurants, people staying generally away from you, but also the rise of the micro-wedding.

As with all the new normals, micro-weddings came about as a need rather than a want – an adaptation to the rules and a smaller version of the ideal. But quickly, a lot of people realised the value of going small.

For some, it became less of an, "Oh fuck, I've got to un-invite a whole bunch of people" and more of an, "Ooh, now I can afford more stuff".

So what's a micro-wedding? Unlike its big sister, the 'intimate/small wedding', you're looking at under 20 of your favourite people for a micro-wedding. Bigger than an elopement, smaller than a housewarming party.

And what are some of the reasons you might consider having a micro- rather than a macro-wedding?

You find large weddings a bit intimidating

Not everyone relishes the idea of being the centre of attention, even on one of the most important days of your life. Maybe it's also that you find the idea of planning something so huge a bit overwhelming and would, frankly, rather not.

You want to spend less in general

Perhaps budget is a concern and the idea that every wedding guest has a Sims-like money icon floating above their heads makes you want to cut that guest list way down.

You want to spend your money on the details rather than the head-count

Having fewer people to feed and water means you can create amazing tablescapes that would otherwise be spread across ten tables or add more personal touches to the day relevant to each guest.

Rather than restrict, a micro-wedding gives budget freedom.

You are conscious of the environmental impact of larger weddings

It's hard to get away from but in most cases the bigger the wedding the bigger the carbon footprint – from the guest travel to the food waste – so reducing the headcount may mean you can reduce your impact on the environment.

You want to spend quality time with your faves

It can be tricky to spend more than a few minutes with each guest when you have an average to larger sized wedding but when you reduce your guest list to 20 or less, you have all dang day to celebrate and enjoy quality time with them.

You're headed further afield

This just often makes more sense. A manageable group of less than 20 just works better for a destination wedding, even if you're just going somewhere in the UK. Fewer people to ask to travel, more options available to you for overnight stays and the wedding day itself.

Okay, so you're now sold on a micro-wedding! Now what?

For starters, you can pretty much carry on reading this book and just apply all your learning to 20 people rather than 120.

Many of the principles are the same – you still need to find a venue, plan the ceremony, invite people, find suppliers, feed people, dress up and show up. Just because it's small doesn't mean it doesn't have to be DETAILED!

But be aware that the typical format that works for the average-sized wedding may not work for a micro one. It's harder to imagine a group of 15 spending hours on the dance floor. It might make sense to bring in some more passive entertainment such as cabaret, stand-up, sleight-of-hand magic and the like.

Keep it shorter, keep it sweeter and get creative with the flow of the day, because you can.

MAKING THAT PAPER: WHAT YOU NEED TO KNOW ABOUT STATIONERY

Announcement! There is so much more to wedding stationery than just the invites!

If you go weak at the knees for pretty paper, that's probably music to your ears. For the rest of you it's just an extra line in the budget to consider, but listen up, doubters – effective information during the planning and on the day itself can save you hours and wrinkles in questions, confusion and the general herding of people.

Let's break it down. Starting with the invitations, the four questions you'll be asking yourself about now are:

1. When should we send the invitations out?

2. How many do we need?

3. What information do we need to include?

4. What tone of voice should we use?

Aim to get your save the dates out 6-7 months before your wedding so it's in your guests' diaries (longer if it's a destination wedding and flights/accommodation need to be considered). Follow up with your invites about 3-4 months before the big day.

You only need one invite per guest group so count up your singletons (decide if they get a plus one), couples and family groups rather than your total guest list and add a few extra just in case.

Remember to keep some spares of your printed invites and bring them on the day. Your photographer can take some amazing professional compositions of your invites with other elements of your decor.

When it comes to information, it's always better to have too much than not enough. That way, you can avoid any pesky questions on dress code, gift list, parking and so on. Here's our handy checklist of what you should include:

Wedding Day

✦ The who, what and where of the day, that's you and your partner, the wedding and location

✦ Make it clear if the invite is a plus one or plus kids

✦ Timings so guests know when to arrive and when they can be expected to be chucked out

✦A rough schedule if you have it so guests have an idea of what the day entails

Travel + Accommodation

✦Any travel between venues that either you're arranging or you need your guests to sort out for themselves

✦Directions, parking information and a map if possible

✦Taxi numbers for the late night revellers

✦Nearby hotel options

FAQS

✦Gift list, if there is one and if so what is it

✦Dress code – yes, we know your guests will scrub up for your wedding, but it's always worth indicating how formal it is so they know if they should crack out their fascinator

RSVP

✦A means to RSVP – this could be an email address, reply cards or their own personal carrier pigeon, your guests just need someway to communicate with you

✦Dietary requirements or meal choices

✦ And don't forget a deadline for RSVPs. Caterers will need final numbers at least a week before, so aim for a month prior to that date to give you some time to chase up the slackers

Another pro tip, number the back of all your RSVP cards and guestlist, to account for someone forgetting to put their name on the card, or for someone having illegible doctor's handwriting

So you know what you need to say - but do you know how to say it? Your invitations should have a certain tone of voice, and these will, obviously, set the tone for your wedding. See the next page for some examples.

TRADITIONAL

JUDY AND JACK GELLER
REQUEST THE PLEASURE OF YOUR
COMPANY AT THE MARRIAGE
OF THEIR DAUGHTER

MONICA GELLER

TO

CHANDLER BING

SON OF
NORA BING AND CHARLES BING

MAY 15TH 2022
TWO O'CLOCK IN THE AFTERNOON

THE NED, LONDON
RECEPTION TO FOLLOW

FORMAL

THE HONOUR OF YOUR
PRESENCE IS REQUESTED AT
THE MARRIAGE OF

MONICA GELLER

AND

CHANDLER BING

2PM, MAY 15TH 2022
ARRIVAL FROM 1PM

THE PRINCES DOME
THE NED, 27 POULTRY, LONDON

DINNER & DANCING TO
FOLLOW

CASUAL

MONICA GELLER

AND

CHANDLER BING

ARE GETTING HITCHED
PLEASE JOIN THEM TO CELEBRATE
THEIR MARRIAGE

2PM, MAY 15TH 2022
ARRIVAL AT 1.30PM

THE PRINCES DOME
THE NED, LONDON

PERSONALITY

HE'S NOT SCARED OF COMMITMENT
ANYMORE, WE'RE GETTING MARRIED!

MONICA & CHANDLER

INVITE YOU TO THE CLEANEST AND
MOST ORGANISED WEDDING
YOU'LL EVER GO TO

2PM, MAY 15TH 2022

AT THE NED, LONDON

PSST, WE'RE RUNNING A SWEEPSTAKE
ON WHAT TIME CHANDLER WILL FREAK
OUT. SEND BACK YOUR NOMINATED
DAY AND TIME WITH YOUR RSVP

Wedding websites

If paper isn't your thing (or you're mindful of the environment) you can have a wedding website instead. The majority of the above information can be hosted on there and you can direct your guests to it on the save the date or invitation.

On-the-day stationery

It's never too early to think about the stationery you might need on the day. It's each to their own here, but typically wedding stationery includes:

✦ Order of service

✦ Table plan or escort cards (these are cards that have your name and table on but you pick your seat when you get there)

✦ Place cards (to match up to the table plan)

✦ Table numbers or names

✦ Menus (food and sometimes bar)

And don't forget your signage. Imagine 100 people in a venue they've never been in before. Now imagine that at least half of them have had one mojito too many and you're trying to move them so you can stick to a schedule and eat on time. Trust us – you'll need signage!

Helpful ones include an order of the day so guests know what's happening at any given time and some directional signs - there's no point having a chill-out area or photo booth if your guests don't know where to find it.

He Said/She Said: Supplier Edition

Kelly from **White Cottage Weddings** says: "Don't be scared to let your personality into your stationery, even if you've opted for the most formal affair, talk to your stationer about how your stationery can best reflect you. Don't be afraid to shop off the shelf and explore independent studios. There are so many great stationers out there and Pinterest and Instagram are awash with choice, but can get overwhelming. Narrow down the options with more relevant hashtags, #minimalistsavethedate, #illustratedweddingmap, that sort of thing.

Above all, love your stationery and take care when choosing the right designer for the job. When the day is over, it's one of the few things that you can keep and display forever so it's worth your time, attention and investment."

DESIGN TIME: FINDING YOUR WEDDING STYLE

In the age of Pinterest and Instagram, couples have more choice than ever when it comes to wedding day ideas. It can be very easy to lose yourself in all the options. So how can you wade through it all and find your wedding style?

Here are a few things to consider when you're furiously pinning away.

Your location

Think about *where* you're getting married. Barn, ballroom, greenhouse or garden – it doesn't always have to define the design of your day but it can definitely help with setting the tone.

Think about design ideas that complement or contrast your venue without clashing. For example, lean into your stately home surroundings with an English garden party marquee or contrast with a bold, rich colour palette and a Moroccan vibe. Go vintage glam in a formal London hotel venue or modern with a neon, geometric-inspired twist.

Casual or formal?

Your design choices will be narrowed down when you think about whether you imagine your wedding day James Bond formal, Ed Sheeran casual or something in-between.

What kind of atmosphere speaks best to you both as a couple? Do you like to host dinner parties and get super-fancy dressed up, or casual BBQs with friends? Whichever option you go for, that level of formality will carry through all the aspects of your wedding, from the invitations to the place settings.

Colour and motif

Colours are the bedrock of wedding design. It's the easiest way to thread all the elements of your wedding together. There are no rules when it comes to building your colour palette.

You can pick your favourite colours, work with the seasons, go bold or keep it soft and romantic.

The options are endless, but here's a little inspo to get you started.

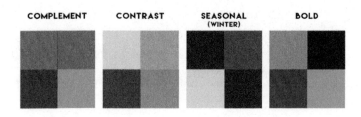

A motif is another design element that can pull your whole look together. Whether it is a monogram, a pattern or a shape that means something to you, it can show up anywhere from the cake to the dance floor to the invitations and the menus. But don't go mad - if you slap it everywhere it will look like you're running a conference. Choose three-to-four key places to show it off.

Look outside the wedding world

The most original, awesome wedding designs come about when couples look elsewhere for inspiration and focus on their shared passions and interests - be it films, travel or childhood nostalgia. A wedding is a chance to show your personalities.

Look around the home. The way you decorate, the furniture you've got, the glassware in your cupboards - this should give you a better indication of what you like more than any digital pinboard could. Only then will you find a wedding style where guests say, "Wow, only they could've had a wedding like this".

STOP TO SMELL THE FLOWERS
(& OTHER PRETTY THINGS)

For most couples, the next step after figuring out their wedding style is to start a mood board. You can get down and dirty with the specifics (like actual names of flowers or exactly what cut glass tumblers you want on the tables) or you can just start pulling a collage of images together that you're drawn to and making notes about what exactly you like about them.

When we're working with couples on design, we start with a big Powerpoint or Word/Pages document with pages that cover the following:

✦ Colours, textures and vibe with some key images to illustrate (eg. hunter green and pale pink, wood and copper, industrial botanical)

✦ Ceremony inspiration (backdrop ideas, flowers, format)

✦ Reception inspiration (tabletops, linen colours, glassware, and so on)

✦ Stationery ideas (from invites all the way to signage on the day)

✦ Any other key details or personal touches you want to include

COLOURS + TEXTURES

Magical and cosy but elegant and design-led. Lush, grounding greenery with natural woods and copper details. Abstract pops of oranges and pinks for a playful side of the day and to reflect a joint love of art.

If a full-on 'style notes document' isn't your idea of fun (to each their own…), start a Pinterest board that has sections for everything and add comments stating what you like/what you would change in a certain image.

This document then serves as a fancy blueprint for any suppliers you start talking to, and then BAM – everyone knows what you're trying to achieve. Plus, it'll win you major points for being a brilliantly organised bride or groom.

But also, don't worry *at all* if your Pinterest board only has five random photos of bouquets or your style doc has a few pages of ideas without a common thread. Any supplier worth their salt – from planners to florists to lighting companies – will use whatever you have as a springboard to make suggestions and help you design something amazing, unique and 100% you.

Seasonal flowers

Maybe you're the kind of person who already knows their dahlia from their foxgloves (hello, Gardener's Question Time), but if you're not even sure if we just named two flowers, read on.

A common mistake couples often make is forgetting that flowers are seasonal – not all flowers will be around for your wedding. You might love a peony, but if your wedding is in the middle of Autumn you'll need to go back to the drawing board.

Below, you'll find a few examples of what's typically available in each season in the UK, though this list is not exhaustive and not always a science since year-on-year availability ebbs and flows.

SPRING

Peonies Roses Ranunculus
Hydrangeas Tulips Orchids
Daffodils Anemones Blossom
Narcissi Lily of the Valley

SUMMER

Roses Peonies Delphinium
Stocks Snapdragons Sunflowers
Marigolds Foxgloves

AUTUMN

Dahlias Hydrangeas Roses
Freesias Lilies
Orchids Anemones Amaryllis

WINTER

Anemones   Hyacinths   Winter camellias   Delphinium Roses   Poinsettias
Chrysanthemums Orchids

Table sizes

How many guests can you fit around a table?

Nope, not the set-up to a joke, but a very useful cheat sheet for knowing what options you have available to you when it comes to seating your guests and designing the layout of your wedding meal.

Stick to the lowest number to give guests the most elbow room, especially if you're planning a table with a lot of glassware and flatware.

Choice of chair usually factors into this number too – some chairs are slimmer than others so you can afford to squeeze more onto the tables.

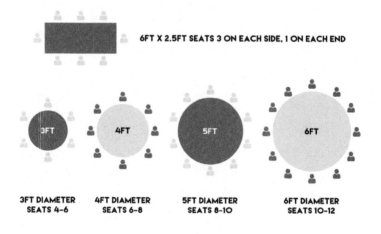

6FT X 2.5FT SEATS 3 ON EACH SIDE, 1 ON EACH END

3FT DIAMETER
SEATS 4-6

4FT DIAMETER
SEATS 6-8

5FT DIAMETER
SEATS 8-10

6FT DIAMETER
SEATS 10-12

Also consider table size and decor choices when it comes to your menu planning. If you plan on having a lot of family-style/sharing platters, you might consider a slightly larger round or wider long table to accommodate both food and centrepieces.

A note on table plans

Ah, the emotional game of Tetris that is the wedding table plan. No one's family and friend groups are so perfect that they work in neat little groups of ten – there's just no freakin' way.

So if you are facing a fun little game of 'who can't sit next to who', we have a few handy tips to make the game a little easier to play!

Map it out

Go low-tech for your first few goes – use pencil and paper, or sticky notes, before graduating to anything more permanent, and *definitely* don't go to print until you really have to.

To group or not to group

Lots of people will make sense to group together – uni friends, distant family, colleagues – but there will always be stragglers. Resist the urge to put all the odd people on one table unless you have to, instead try to fit a few people in with current groups that you think might get along. Your neighbour couple might have the perfect sense of humour for work friends; your cousin and his wife you've never met might have a lot in common with some of your friends from school - you get the picture.

<u>Modern families</u>

Whether it's divorced parents or people who have had a falling out – you have two options. One is to figure out a seating plan that means those people won't have each other in their line of sight during dinner, OR tell everyone to suck it up for one day and play nice as a gift to you.

Be amenable and considerate to an extent, but if you find yourself bending over backwards for a handful of particularly difficult people, lay down the law and issue an ultimatum - sit where we put you or eat outside...

<u>Kids</u>

If you are having kids at your dinner, depending on the ages you might decide to put them all together – give them their own kid's menu and some table games.

If they are at the table, remember to ask the parents if you need to get them a highchair from the caterer and factor that into your table plan.

Numbers vs names

Ah, the eternal debate. Sure, numbers are easier and more logical but they can also indicate hierarchy (table 15 are throwing shade at you from way back there). Names require a bit more thought and creativity, but they eliminate any question of importance.

About face

Once you have figured out who is sitting on which table, then it's time to consider where on the table each person should sit.

You may not think it matters, but consider who is on the table – if you have any older guests or those with disabilities, make sure they are facing the head table. When it comes to speeches and generally just looking adoringly at how bangin' you look, you won't want them to be straining or cricking their neck for long periods of time.

Head table dilemmas

The head table can be one of the trickiest parts of table plan planning. Especially if you have a complicated set up – parents who aren't together, are with other partners, or a veritable horde of siblings or bridesmaids.

Depending on your venue, your head table can be as big or as small as you want. A super long, double sided table works for big wedding parties. Or to be diplomatic, sit just with your parents, your best man and your maid of honour.

Some couples even opt for a sweetheart table with just the two of them – not that hard for couples who spent a year locked down and looking at each other over endless takeaway.

But perhaps sitting with your parents, best man and maid of honour - the traditional trifecta - doesn't work for you. Like many traditions, it emerged in a different time and for different reasons. Why not just sit on a table with your closest friends? They have the best bants, anyway.

WEDDING FOOD & DRINK: THE FEEDING OF THE 150

Food and drink is one of the biggest and best ways you can really inject your own ideas and personality into the day. It makes a huge impression – and thank goodness it does, because it takes up a fucking huge part of your budget…

Food style

The kind of food you serve and the way you serve it often comes down to three things – your venue, your budget and the vibe of the day. So what are your options?

Canapés

Typically served after the ceremony with drinks. A little snack to tide guests over while they mingle and take photos. Great for lining stomachs on a hot day when alcohol is in play…

Bowl food

If you're having a standing reception instead of a sit-down meal, bowl food is a great idea. It's food designed for interacting and mingling while you eat – miniature dishes of your favourite foods. It's great for variety, and more substantial for your upstanding guests than canapés.

Afternoon tea

A more relaxed wedding meal option, great if you're having an early ceremony and want to serve something lighter and more 'picky' for your guests afterwards.

BBQ / hog roast

One of the more cost effective ways of feeding the masses, but it's also a great crowd pleaser. Brilliant for evening food to soak up the alcohol.

Plated meal

The most obvious option and one that many wedding venues will include in their packages as standard. It's a little more formal, but you have the peace of mind of knowing everyone is getting enough food. Find ways to fit this format in with your style by choosing a menu that reflects your own taste and favourite flavours.

Family style dining

Somewhere between a plated meal and a buffet is family style dining. A tabletop buffet option where guests have sharing platters and a mix of options available to them.

Buffet

A self-serve heaven – everything displayed beautifully on long tables and guests can choose what they would like and how much to eat. A flexible option, especially if you have picky eaters or want to have a real range of foods available without spending a ton.

Self-serve stations

Serving stations are a bit like a buffet, but more for peripheral foods found in post-ceremony snacks, an evening buffet or a sweets table.

Food trucks and street food

There are so many amazing caterers and cuisines available in this format now. It's a great way to do evening food, but if it's for your main meal it's worth noting it takes a lot longer to feed everyone this way.

Remember, if you're going for a super casual food truck / food delivery route, make sure you think about how it will be served as if you're expecting wait staff to handle it you may be disappointed.

He Said/She Said: Supplier Edition

Julie Crump, from award-winning caterers **Caviar & Chips**, says: "Food is something that brings people together, helps break the ice and who doesn't love talking about their favourite meal or cocktail?! Our advice would be choose food and drink that you love. Don't worry about whether some of your friends won't like one of your canapés or if some of your relatives won't like the dessert. It's your big day and you'll enjoy it so much more by doing it the way you want to.

Make sure you get to try your menu with your caterers and understand what it will look like, how it will be served and what your guests will experience. This will give you peace of mind that your guests will have an amazing day with you, no matter what's on their plate or in their glass!"

Questions to ask your wedding caterers

If you're in a position to choose your own caterers, either from a venue's recommended shortlist or from scratch, it can be hard to know how to whittle it down to your top choices. So see our handy list of questions to ask in our master planning template when you're chatting to or meeting with prospective catering companies for your day.

Trimming the fat on your catering budget

If you're on a tight budget, how do you bring costs down without starving your guests?

Choices, choices and more choices...

It's great to have a range of options when you go out for a meal, but your wedding isn't a restaurant. You can limit the number of options your guests have for your wedding meal and save you time, stress and – more importantly – cold hard cash.

Streamlining

Save money by merging some of your meal times. Consider serving chunkier, more substantial canapés which can double up as a starter followed by a two course meal.

Go seasonal

Ask your caterer what's in season for your wedding date so they can buy local and not have to charge you to import expensive, out-of-season produce for a dish you liked the look of.

Cut loose

It's a harsh truth, but every wedding guest has a price on their head. If you squint, you can almost see the floating number above them as they are walking around, drinking your wine. Every plus one, third cousin and former colleague you invite adds up-wards of £50 to your catering alone. Once you add in the chairs, linens, plates and staff you start to wonder if you still want to invite *all* your old school friends you haven't spoken to in years.

Drinks

Ah the litmus test for a good party: the booze!

What, how much and when to serve drinks at a wed-ding can send some couples into a bit of a daze.

Who's buying?

First question – who is going to be in charge of buy-ing? Depending on your venue, you may have the option of either bringing in your own or having the catering team take care of it.

Bringing in your own might incur a corkage charge – the fee your venue or caterer will charge per bottle, per head or as a one off payment, for handling and serving your alcohol.

If you do decide to buy your own alcohol, you can take advantage of great bulk discounts from certain warehouses and you can take your time over the course of planning to spot good offers on your favourites to stock up.

Many wine merchants will also offer a sale or return, so you have the peace of mind of buying more than you need and being able to get a refund for any un-opened boxes you have left over.

Booze maths

So if you're buying your own booze, how much do you need so you don't over-order – or worse – run dry?

Arrival drinks

✦ There are six full glasses of prosecco, Champagne or sparkling wine in a standard 750ml bottle

✦ Allow for two glasses per adult for an hour long drinks reception – at least 40 bottles for 120 drinking guests. Add another glass if it's going on for longer

1 BOTTLE CHAMPAGNE   **6 GLASSES**

✦ If you go for bucks fizz or another Champagne cocktail, you can get 10-12 glasses out of a bottle

Meal drinks

✦ There are up to six glasses in a standard bottle of wine

✦ Allocate half a bottle of wine (three glasses) per guest and have enough for an extra glass if your meal might stretch longer than 2.5 hours

1 GUEST   **1/2 BOTTLE WINE**   **2 HOURS**

+ If the bottles are left on the table, you may need to allocate more per person, since self-serving guests do tend to be more generous pourers

+ Typically, the preference between red or white is 50/50 amongst guests, but in the warmer months it will swing more towards white, or even rosé

Speeches and toasts

+ Allow one glass per person for the speeches, if they are all in one go. Top ups may be needed if they go over 30 mins, or are in two batches

+ And if you're going for shots - leave a small bottle on each table for self-serve!

+ Don't feel you have to have a specific drink for speeches, most guests are happy to toast with whatever they've got in front of them at the time and you can avoid added time, cost and waste on to your day if you skip this step

Evening bar

1 GUEST   1 HOUR   1 DRINK

✦ A good rule of thumb is to estimate one drink per guest every hour after the meal, so calculate how many hours of drinking you'll have once dessert is cleared - typically three or four

✦ In general, guests drink more red wine at an evening reception than during the day

✦ Assume each bottle of spirit has 18 servings in it with a mixer

1 BOTTLE SPIRITS   **18 SHOTS**

✦ And don't forget your extras like garnishes, mixers and ice!

We have it on good authority from caterer pals that guests rarely drink as much as you expect and the average is seven drinks for the whole day, of course some will drink a lot more and some a lot less so think about who's coming. Have you got a crowd of drinkers or are they a bit more reserved?

A guide to cake

And so, to the centrepiece of your wedding reception! No it's not you – it's your cake. But before you get caught up in icing designs and flavour profiles, let's get back to basics. Here's what you need to know.

Numbers

The bigger the cake, the bigger the bill – so there might need to be a compromise between your budget, the number of people you expect to feed and the style of cake you want.

How many guests do you think will even eat the cake? Depending on when you serve it, you might find some people just aren't in the mood for cake. To save you wasting food (and money), don't account for every single guest – enough cake to feed 85% will do the trick.

If you plan to save the top tier of your cake for any reason, make sure you factor that into the total slices you'll have remaining.

You've also got to think about what *size* slice you're talking about. As if you've not got enough on your metaphorical plate.

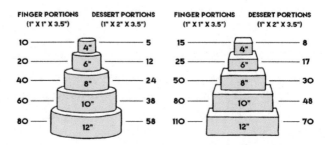

FINGER PORTIONS (1" X 1" X 3.5")	DESSERT PORTIONS (1" X 2" X 3.5")	FINGER PORTIONS (1" X 1" X 3.5")	DESSERT PORTIONS (1" X 2" X 3.5")
10 — 4" — 5		15 — 4" — 8	
20 — 6" — 12		25 — 6" — 17	
40 — 8" — 24		50 — 8" — 30	
60 — 10" — 38		80 — 10" — 48	
80 — 12" — 58		110 — 12" — 70	

Finger portions are usually for when a little bit of cake is served alongside other desserts, or coffee in the evening. A dessert portion is when the cake is the main dessert (a good money-saving route) so needs to be a bit more substantial.

If you want the illusion of a larger cake but don't want to pay for one, you can include a fake layer. Cut the real layer for the photo op, and once the cake gets whisked off for cutting up, add in some sheet cake (behind the scenes cake in the kitchen no one sees). Your guests will be none the wiser and you'll have some money back in your pocket. Alternatively, go for a showy double-height single-tier cake for cutting, but have a prepared sheet cake for serving afterwards to make up the numbers.

If you want to avoid waste – and who doesn't? – offer takeaway boxes to make sure all cake goes to a good home.

He Said/She Said: Supplier Edition

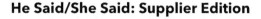 Marianna Vaki from **Whisk & Drizzle** says: "The most important thing in the first instance is to think about whether having a bespoke cake is a priority for you. It's absolutely fine if it isn't and plenty of bakeries out there will make delicious wedding cakes you can pick 'off the shelf', which will be a lot cheaper than anything bespoke. If a unique cake is important to you then my advice is to choose the right cake maker and trust them fully.

Do some research before enquiring - even if you don't have any design ideas in mind, you will still know if you like a cake maker's style and portfolio. Once you've picked your cake maker, trust them with the design and process. They know what will work and what will not, so take their advice on board, give them some creative freedom and you'll have a winner."

Alternatives

And what if you don't actually like cake? Don't have it! Look for alternatives like doughnut towers, a full on dessert grazing table or stacked cheese to cut instead - it's a day about you and what you want to serve so don't lean into tradition if you just don't like cake that much (weirdo).

ATTIRE: I'VE GOT NOTHING TO WEAR & OTHER STORIES

When you've got no frame of reference for choosing a wedding dress it can seem a bit daunting. It's hard enough to buy a good pair of jeans, never mind an all-important wedding outfit. And don't get us *started* on swimwear.

If you're going for the classic white dress, there are a ton of dress silhouettes to look at, and our first piece of advice is to go into a bridal shop and try on one of each. Even if you think you'd never, *ever* wear that particular style - try it on, for two reasons:

1. It narrows down what you do want and either cements your existing ideas or opens your eyes to new possibilities

2. When else do you you get the chance to try on multiple wedding dresses? Cue 'cheesy dress trying-on montage'

Wedding dress shopping is so often a too-many-cooks scenario. Try to do this on your own, or with one tactful person you really trust, so you form your own opinion before you start the real search.

<u>Massive</u> caveat on the whole big white dress thing

Though this chapter covers mainly the idea of a dress-dress, there is absolutely no need to go down the white dress route at all if it's not your style. More than ever, women are going for show-stopping outfits that a) aren't white and b) aren't even a dress. Jumpsuits or tailored white suits are increasingly popular; bold-coloured ballgowns are always an incredible surprise. Go for styles and colours that flatter your shape and that you feel good in. Don't limit yourself!

Research, research, research

Look at different designers and narrow down your favourites. Find out where they are stocked and see if there is anything local to you, a friend or family member. Most shops won't stock the whole range so if there is a particular dress you like, find out if they have it or if they can order it in from the designer (they might charge for this but it'll be deductible if you buy).

You can also make appointments at a few different shops and just start trying on the stock they have in and see if you find one you like.

When trying on dresses, do it in well-fitting underwear, preferably nude. A dress will sit differently if you're wearing a bra that's two sizes too small. Don't worry about shoes – the boutique will have some you can try on with the dress.

Don't forget about sample sales, especially if there is a particular designer you like. A sample sale is when designers sell the remaining dresses at the end of the season at a lower price. You can get yourself a real bargain. Bear in mind, though, that sample sizes are exactly that - samples. So they often won't have anything for brides taller than 5'10 or for bigger busts. If you find something that can be altered, make sure you factor that into the total cost. Samples have also been in shops for months being handled and walked across floors so you'll want to get it professionally cleaned before you wear it.

You've found the one!

Once you've found your dress it's all about the fitting. The shop will order a dress in your size. Over the next six months or so you'll need to have a couple of fittings to adjust the length and any other parts of the dress that need taking in, up or out.

DON'T FORGET YOUR SHOES on your first fitting so they can get the length right.

Hidden costs

Sometimes, shops will charge you to order in dresses, appointments and tailoring. And remember to factor in travel costs for fittings if you choose not to buy your dress locally.

If you like your friends, put them in nice dresses

Once you've got your dress sorted it's time to think about the people that are going up the aisle before you. There are four key things to bear in mind:

1. Pick a dress or dresses that complements your outfit

2. Pick a colour or colours that work with your wedding style

3. Pick something they'll be comfortable wearing

4. They don't actually have to match

That's right folks, gone are the days of matchy-matchy bridesmaid dresses in pastel colours. You can go for different fits, colours and lengths to keep your bridesmaids happy. Narrow down some options and get their opinion on what they like best.

DID YOU KNOW...?

In medieval times, bridesmaids wore the same dresses as the bride to confuse evil spirits - that's one of the reasons bridesmaids traditionally wear matching outfits.

You: Fancy risking your life and soul to be my bridesmaid?
Bridesmaid: Erm.
You: There's cake!
Bridesmaid: Oh, well bloody count me in then.

Etiquette

This often trips people up. There are no hard and fast rules on what you should buy versus what your bridesmaids should buy since everyone's financial situation is different. However, if you have picked their dress for them it seems fair for you to cover the cost. Shoes and accessories are more fluid and it's up to you if you want to pay for these as it's likely your bridesmaids will be able to wear them again. Hair and makeup is also something you don't have to pay for unless you want to. Hopefully your bridesmaids will appreciate the cost of your wedding and won't begrudge paying for their own make up if they choose to have it done professionally.

All men look good in a suit

But how are you going to pick one?! You need to consider style, fit, colour and season to keep your groom and his best men looking suave until after midnight.

Wedding suits typically come in four styles. You need to decide what type of wedding you're having and match the suit to that style.

Morning Suit - This is the most formal option available for grooms. Traditionally worn with a top hat, striped trousers and a waistcoat, you generally see this style at traditional church weddings or very formal civil ceremonies.

Tails - This is less formal than a morning suit but still pretty full on. The classic tail coat has two long tails at the back and should be worn with braces, a white shirt, waistcoat and cravat.

Black Tie - Only for formal, elegant or evening weddings, the black tie screams glamour, so if you're having a festival-style wedding it's probably best avoided.

Lounge Suit - The most popular style is a classic everyday-style suit, which can be enhanced by a matching waistcoat or cravat. It can be tailored to fit so it sits perfectly and it's a suit that can be worn again.

When it comes to the fit the main options are:

Regular - classic style in a comfortable fit with room for extra movement

Slim - a fitted suit ideal for those with a slimmer physique

Tailored - a more streamlined look and a midway option which allows more movement than a regular fit

Remember to consider the season and location of the wedding. We know English weather can be un-predictable but if you're plumping for an August bank holiday wedding and the suit is heavy wool, chances are you're going to get warm!

Ready for my close-up

It's not just what you're wearing that you need to consider, but how you look on the day. Most brides choose to book a hair-and-make up artist; even if you're a dab hand at 'your look', it's nice to feel pampered.

All hair-and-makeup artists will offer a trial for a fee. This is well worth the cost.

As part of the trial you spend a few hours together talking through and trying what you'd like for the day and by the end of the session you will have agreed your style. This is great for anxious brides. If you've already spent some time with your hair-and-makeup artist and you trust them, it's one less thing to worry about on the day.

On the morning of the wedding, wear a shirt or robe when having your makeup and hair done so you don't have to pull anything over your head when you change - but be aware whatever you wear will be in the photos, so choose wisely!

Top trial tips

Wear a top that's a similar colour to your dress. It gives you a better idea of how the make up will work with your wedding dress.

Even if you don't usually wear much makeup you will need to have more slapped on for it to last through the day and to show up in pictures. However, that doesn't mean you should be contoured to Kardashian perfection. Be honest with your make up artist: if it's too much, tell them and they can tone it down - that's the beauty of having a trial.

Make sure you know what lipstick and/or gloss you're wearing so you can buy it yourself for touch ups throughout the day.

He Said/She Said: Supplier Edition

Jo Adams, founder of **Hair & Makeup Atelier**, says: "Don't wing it! How you feel on your wedding day is SO important! And it's equally important that you feel relaxed with your makeup artist while you're getting ready.

Nailing your most fabulous version of 'you' isn't something you should leave open to interpretation on the most important day of your life. Choose an artist whose style and personality you feel an affinity for, but also be prepared to do some homework. Taking the time to think about your likes and dislikes or collecting pictures will really help your artist get a feel for your look - you don't want to leave it to the wedding day to find out you and your artist have a very different idea of what a smokey eye looks like!"

PHOTO + VIDEO: YOU PAID A LOT OF MONEY FOR ONE DAY, BETTER COLLECT EVIDENCE

It doesn't matter if you stick to water all day or if you're downing sambucas at the bar — your wedding day will still be a blur by the following week. A nice blur, but a blur nonetheless. So getting photographs and/or video of the occasion is a smart move.

How much?

Wedding photographers and videographers vary in budget depending on their experience, your location and the number of hours they're doing. You can pay anything from £500 to £5000. However, if photography and videography are very important to you try to ring-fence at least £1500 each.

The shot list

Every photographer prefers to have a 'shot list' to work from on the day, even documentary photographers. By 'shot list' we just mean the posed photographs and any non-obvious specifics; not a full list of every single image, that would be insane. Trust your photographer to capture the day, that's what you hired them for.

Let friends and family know they'll be in the photos so they are easy to find when you need them. Speaking of which, delegate the job of rounding everyone up so you're not waiting for your mum while she's getting stuck into the Pimms.

Make a note of all the group combinations you don't want to have missed - from the obvious (the couple plus parents) to the unusually specific (the groom with his stepdad and neighbour's dog). It's unlikely your photographer will know your particular family history and all its' quirks, so this is the shot list we're talking about to make sure they don't miss anyone or anything.

Guests and their bloody phones

One of the worst things a wedding photographer and videographer can experience on the day is losing a perfect once-in-a-lifetime shot. Want to know the main reason that happens? Your guests and their phones. That iconic moment when your ceremony ends and you seal it with a kiss - your photographer will likely want to get that amazing shot from the middle of the aisle. BUT when your uncle Al steps out into the aisle to take that same photo with his iPad (it's always a fucking iPad), that moment is gone.

It's getting increasingly popular to set up an unplugged wedding ceremony - ban your guests from taking photos on their devices until after the ceremony and you can let your photographer do their job without worrying about rogue phones.

Heads up

If you are planning some fun surprises for your guests - maybe a fireworks display, singing waiters, or a surprise dance - you *have* to let your photographer and videographer in on those secrets. Those are the moments you don't want them to miss because they didn't know it was happening, including planning their angles to capture the priceless look on your guests' faces!

Connection is key

If you're having both a photographer and a videographer, make sure they've connected before the wedding. They're going to be working alongside each other for the day and they'll need to give way to each other so they can both get the best work for you.

Make sure they communicate so they can do this effectively and you end up with amazing photos and video.

Amateur hour

We've all got a mate who thinks they're the next Annie Leibovitz. They're not, but hey, that's why they're free. If budget is an issue and you've got a friend volunteering to be behind the camera make sure they're briefed the same way you would brief a professional. If they are solely responsible for your wedding photos give them as much information as possible - what you want, what you don't want and the schedule of the day so they can be in the right place at the right time. Maybe get them to lay off the booze until into the evening as well.

ARE YOU NOT ENTERTAINED?

There are so many forms of entertainment you can have at your wedding. A quick Google search will fill you with ideas, so this chapter isn't going to be a list of what the internet can already tell you – just essential advice on sound and lighting for the big day.

If the thought of Aunt Sharon leading the conga round the reception fills you with dread, never fear. As well as sharing your favourite songs with your music act, you can have a 'No Play' playlist to keep her feet firmly under the table.

If you're on a tight budget and can't afford to book a band, DJs are typically cheaper – there are fewer people to pay, and fewer suppliers to feed. If you're on a really tight budget, put together a playlist – Spotify has a crossfade option so you aren't left with bouts of silence between songs.

Your venue should have a PA system (do check) for your playlists, but prick your ears up for five absolute gold-dust tips on playlists here:

1. Make sure your playlist is downloaded in case the WiFi drops out, and put your phone on airplane

mode/sign out of all video call platforms, should an absolute idiot call on your wedding day

2. Write your pin/password down for your venue/planner so if your phone/laptop locks they can get back in to access the playlist

3. Hand over the playlist in good time - that may mean a member of your wedding party arriving a bit early with it in hand - so a quick sound check can be done and it can be cued up properly

4. Separate your music into playlists so whoever is operating it on the day knows your entrance and exit music for the ceremony

5. And finally (thank us later for this), if you have a newer iPhone/Mac please check that the venue has an adapter to plug it in to the PA system, or bring your own.

All of the lights and other Kayne West songs

Whatever you think of the man, his songs pack a dance floor, but we digress - this section is about lighting...

We cannot stress enough how much the right lighting can set the atmosphere for every part of your day. Most venues will include a set number of uplighters in the hire – for the uninitiated this is a light that sits on the floor and illuminates the wall/pillar it is next to. These are great, take as many as the venue will give you. However, most venues will just provide a standard look for day and night.

One of the best pieces of advice we as planners can give you is THINK ABOUT YOUR LIGHTING!!!

Do some research online and pick out images for all parts of your day to show to your venue and/or planner so they can advise on how to achieve that look and the likely cost involved.

Your DJ/band may have access to more lighting that they can bring in and set up for you, from additional uplighters to laser lights/haze (these look amazing, but the smoke alarms will need to be briefly disconnected so make sure the venue is made aware). Potentially what you want to achieve may involve bringing in an additional production team, especially if it's a dry hire venue.

If you want value for money, never underestimate the power of candles for the ceremony and dinner. There are so many different styles and colours available for a variety of budgets. The only key question to ask your venue is, do you allow naked flame? If the answer is yes then buy all the candles you can get your wedding mitts on. If it's no, then battery operated candles are a good alternative – but these tend to look best in holders so the 'flame' is hidden.

Sound and lighting may feel a bit overwhelming because it's technical, but if you've done the due diligence to find a good venue and suppliers they will be invaluable in helping you create the look and feel of the day you want.

Bodies on the dance floor

If you need to hire in a dance floor or mark out an area for dancing, how much space do you need?

Typically you can assume about 30-40% of your guests are throwing some shapes at any given time, but round this up if you've got a lot of party animals coming, or down if it's an older audience or you've got other activities going on at the same time. Not all companies hire out the same dance floor sizes so this isn't an exact science, but here's a rough guide:

100 guests = 40 dancers = 12x12ft dance floor
150 guests = 60 dancers = 15x15ft dance floor
200 guests = 80 dancers = 18x18ft dance floor
250 guests = 100 dancers = 20x20ft dance floor

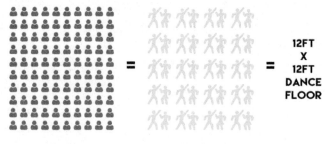

100 GUESTS   40 DANCING GUESTS

WEDDING TRADITIONS TO TRASH (IN OUR OPINION)

Personally, we think there are no hard and fast rules to weddings (apart from those pesky legal ones, they are pretty rigid) and if you want to break traditions and go rulebook-free, well that is fine and dandy with us.

With that in mind we've pulled together a list of traditions that you might expect to have to follow at your wedding but in the words of the immortal Celine Dion we're telling you to 'think twice'.

Not seeing each other the night before

They say, it's bad luck. We say, it's never been cited in a divorce yet! This is a very old tradition, long before cohabitation came along.

Most of you find out if you can cope with your other half's snoring long before you get hitched – why should this night be any different. Enjoy your last night as a betrothed couple.

Old, new, borrowed, blue

You've got a wedding to plan, you haven't got time to find something blue to slip into your garter (and just to be clear, that's another thing to go in the trash pile).

Look, if you've got people around you who firmly believe in this and you don't care either way then fine, go with it, but don't spend your last weeks of engagement trailing the antique shops looking for the perfect something old, it won't make a blind bit of difference to your day.

The receiving line

Way back, the bride's parents traditionally hosted the wedding and this was a way to meet the thousands of people that had been invited.It's not seen as much these days when weddings are a bit less formal. Plus it takes freakin' ages, and you barely get 30 seconds with each person before you're onto the next thing. Just aim to get round everyone during drinks, dinner and in the evening so you can be more relaxed and take your time.

The processional song

Traditionally this was Wagner's Bridal Chorus, but nowadays the shackles have lifted and for a civil service you can strut your stuff down that aisle to anything that isn't a hymn or wildly offensive. This is one of the first parts of the day where you can let your personality shine, so make it count.

Throwing the bouquet

Meant to indicate the next person to get married, we think it's a load of old pish. Having said that, point your camera in that direction if you decide to do it, the results can be hilarious – they might even win you £250 on You've Been Framed (are we showing our age here?).

All-male speeches

Now this is one tradition that *definitely* needs to change and we're seeing that movement already. Lots of brides, mothers of brides/grooms and bridesmaids are now making speeches on the big day. If you want to get up there to say thanks and tell some stories then go for it. Long live equal-opportunity speeches!

GIMME ALL THE GIFTS

Most people will expect (nay, want) to get you a gift for your wedding, so don't feel guilty or uncomfortable about this. Embrace it and give your guests the information they need.

If you are doing a gift list of physical items, make sure you have a good price range on there. Sure, people want to commemorate your new life stage and marital status, but don't take the piss and wipe out their life savings.

If you're asking for money – towards your honeymoon, say – most people are happy to do this; there are websites that can manage this for you. However, these websites *will* take a slice of the pie, so if you want to keep all the money but not give out bank details (which, let's face it, can be pretty vulgar) then consider PayPal as the ultimate hack. Guests can pay directly into your PayPal account via theirs. It's one step removed from a bank transfer, but you keep all the wonga for yourself.

Even if you're primarily asking for money you may be aware of some guests (often older) who would prefer to give a physical gift, in which case you can still register on a gift list for some items. A lot of gift lists now also let you do a split between gifts and honeymoon donations so you have everything in one place.

The language you use when asking for gifts is always important. Match it to the style of your invitations so it doesn't look out of place, but don't be presumptuous. No one has to buy you a gift so consider it information for anyone that wants to rather than a request.

You might be tempted to ignore the gift list completely - don't. Guests will still ask or with no steer they might buy an unwanted present which is a waste of their money. If you genuinely don't want any gifts then nominate a charity for your guests to donate to instead.

And don't forget to provide some sort of container or post box for any cards or gifts that are given to you on the day. Most people feel like they shouldn't turn up to a wedding empty handed, so you can expect a card at least. Make it clear where they can be put on the day and then you or a nominated friend or family member can collect them at the end of the night.

HOW TO NOT HATE
YOUR OWN WEDDING

Planning a wedding is damn stressful, and it can be so incredibly tempting to run off and get hitched under an oak tree in the South of France. But if that's going to be too much for your parents to handle, how do you manage to not resent your own wedding while you're planning it?

Adjust your own timeline

There's no rule about the length of your engagement. A year seems like the average for most couples, but given recent events this has lengthened a lot of engagements. Smaller weddings on home soil will be easier to plan than a large affair or something overseas. Not enough time will leave you stressed. Too much time leaves too many opportunities to change your mind.

Set boundaries

One of the biggest reasons couples will want to elope is the pressure of having to please everyone. The trick is to set boundaries from the outset. Smile and nod at any unsolicited advice and requests, and then calmly explain that the two of you will talk it over and decide together. Then you can bitch about them later.

As we've said before, it can be difficult if you're not the ones paying, and you don't know how much say you can really have in your own wedding. Have an honest conversation with your benefactors as soon as they offer you any money. You need to know what they expect in return, and not be surprised later down the line when you find out more of your mum's friends are coming to the wedding than your own.

Delegate

Yeah sure, this is your day, but that doesn't mean you have to do *everything* yourself.

Getting a wedding planner can be a life-saving option for brides who just want to hand stuff over to a professional (shameless plug). We hire people to wash our cars, fix our clothes and cut our hair. Not because we couldn't do it ourselves, or that we couldn't learn – it's that we don't have the time or the expertise. Why should the most important day of your life be any different?

If professional planning isn't in the budget, ask friends. You'll be surprised at how much people are willing to pitch in. Got a friend with gorgeous handwriting? Set them to work on envelopes. If you know someone who really, weirdly likes spreadsheets (we do), ask them to manage your RSVPs.

Hindsight

In the stress of planning, it's easy to believe the number of peonies in your bouquet or the colour of the uplighters are the most important things in the world.

If that sounds like you, ask yourself - will this make or break the day? Am I going to look back and remember that in ten years? Or even one year? A week?

Ask any #smugmarrieds what elements of the day really stick out in their memory. Then you'll know what to focus on and what to palm off to someone else.

Look at honeymoons

If all else fails, concentrate on the honeymoon. Santorini or Cancun? Sun or ski? Hotel or villa? Now, these are decisions you can get on (full) board with.

Keep that image in your head of just the two of you in a faraway place, sharing a giant bottle of wine and finally able to laugh about how crazy things got in the last few months. If it helps your stress levels, adjust your calendar to countdown to the day you leave on honeymoon, instead of the wedding...

Remember why you're doing this

Look at your partner. Just really look at them. That's why you're doing this. You're planning a wedding because you want to be married to that face forever.

Of course the wedding is important, it's a day to celebrate the start of your lives together but it's one day in a million that you'll get to spend with that person who steals the covers and spends too long on the toilet. What you're really doing is having a marriage launch party and it should be the next 20, 30, 50 years you're looking forward to.

Remember that the next time you're shouting down the phone because your caterer ordered round plates instead of the square ones you saw on that blog.

HOW LONG DOES IT TAKE TO CUT A CAKE (& OTHER SCHEDULE QUESTIONS)

Unless you're a Type A individual who couldn't think of anything more fun that spreadsheets and calculations (like us), the idea of putting together your wedding day schedule is bound to be a little nerve-wracking. How do you even start? How much time does everything need? HOW AM I SUPPOSED TO INSTINCTIVELY KNOW HOW LONG IT TAKES TO CUT A DAMN WEDDING CAKE??

Alright, calm down.

First of all, it's your wedding and you know best about how you want everything to run. You have free rein over what comes after what and when. But flow is important, and scheduling too little or too much time for certain things can lead to either chaos or boredom.

The basics

Best place to start is with the time you want to eat and work backwards from there to your ideal ceremony time (provided you have options and aren't hemmed in by limited registrar slots).

A practical format of the day might be, for example:

✦ Ceremony at 3 pm

✦ Drinks reception and photos at 4 pm

✦ Sit down to dinner at 5:30 pm

✦ Speeches at 7 pm

✦ Dessert at 7:30 pm

✦ Cake cutting and first dance at 8:30 pm

✦ Evening buffet at 10 pm

✦ Dancing, drinking and chatting until 12 pm / 1 am

That way you're feeding yourselves and your guests at a normal (slightly early bird) mealtime, and more importantly you and your wedding party have time to eat before heading out to say I Do. Evening snacks come out at the perfect time between finishing the meal and the end of the night, so you hit guests at 'peak peckish'.

Getting ready

The time you need to get ready the morning of your wedding is usually the most underestimated in the wedding day schedule. It's often very hard to know how quickly your hair and makeup will be done, especially if you're factoring bridesmaids/mothers into the equation.

Work backwards from when you will have to leave for the ceremony, and ask your stylists how much time they think they will need. As a general guide, bridal hair and makeup can take up to two hours, and an additional hour per each bridesmaid or mum.

Leave about an hour for margin of error between being finished and leaving for the ceremony - no one wants to be a rushed bride, but extra time for getting dressed, photos and nerve-calming never hurts!

Ceremony

A civil ceremony will only last about 15 minutes, which is why it's great to add readings and music to lengthen it to 25/30 minutes and make it more personal to you as a couple. Make sure someone (usually an usher) is at the ceremony venue around an hour beforehand to start handing out orders of service (if you are having them) and seat any early arrivals - there are *always* early arrivals.

Reception

Before the wedding breakfast, you typically have a few hours of mingling time with drinks, canapés and entertainment - often called cocktail hour or drinks reception. Remember, the longer you schedule for this, more drinks, canapés and entertainment will be needed.

It's a balancing act of using the drinks reception to get some couples shots, group shots and mingling with your guests without it going on too long that your guests get antsy for dinner. We suggest no longer than 90 minutes before guests are called through for the wedding breakfast.

A three-course wedding breakfast can take roughly two hours, but always consult your caterer for their suggested timings, as it depends on headcount and the way the courses are being served.

Speeches rarely run to time! As a rule of thumb, give 10 minutes to each speaker (but allow 15 in your schedule) especially if you have quite a few. Caterers will love you if you have your starter and main before any speeches and then there is less stress over how long they might take, plus your guests are suitably full of food and drink and more relaxed and ready to listen to some embarrassing stories about you.

Make your own rules

Here's to rulebook-free weddings! There's no reason to stick to traditional wedding day timings unless you really want to. Ceremonies can start any time of the day and your reception doesn't always have to be a sit-down formal meal. Why not have a morning ceremony and a boozy pancake brunch reception? Or a late-night ceremony with a standing cocktail hour reception? Because, you bloody can and it's your day (or night).

IT'S THE FINAL COUNTDOWN (SORRY, NOT SORRY, FOR THE SONG NOW IN YOUR HEAD)

Whether you're a couple who have spent two years or two months planning your celebration, you'll have one thing in common - the final stressful weeks of the home stretch.

One of the most popular wedding-planning services is final weeks and on-the-day coordination. That's for good reason: having someone else step in to 'check your work' and ensure nothing's been missed – as well as take all the final stresses off your shoulders – can be invaluable.

Update and send out the schedule

One of the most time-consuming but all-important elements of the final few weeks is finalising your on-the-day schedule, but don't forget to also include timing and info for the days before and after if it's relevant.

The pre-event information might cover deliveries the day before, family dropping things off at the venue, nail appointments, last-minute pick ups of everything. Post-event should cover when suppliers are coming back to collect any items or dismantle the marquee, and lists of any items you need the caterer/venue to save for you to pick up.

This schedule will mainly be for all your suppliers, and for ease we recommend sending the same one to everyone regardless of the size of their role in the wedding — this avoids having to create individual timelines and causing confusion.

Caterers will have their own timeline of the day, so it's important they have sight of yours well in advance. You don't find out too late that you thought dinner was at 5 pm and they thought it was at 6 pm. You can then finalise the schedule a week or two before so you have a stress free final few days. You might want to copy in your wedding party if you've given them jobs to do on the day.

Remember to use our downloadable and editable master schedule template for a much more detailed version.

Chase RSVPS & dietaries

Check over your guest list and follow up with anyone you need to. Inevitably people change their plans last minute, and you end up adding new guests, taking some guests off and new allergies/intolerances suddenly crop up. Most caterers need the final numbers and seating chart a week before the wedding.

Triple check your furniture hire list to ensure it's reflective of your final headcount. All too often, bookings for things like chairs are made before the final guest list is confirmed; couples find themselves either overpaying for too many unnecessary chairs, or forgetting to increase the order and scrambling for spares.

Make final payments

Your bank balance is about to take a final blow: the majority of your suppliers will request any outstanding balances two to four weeks before the wedding. Make sure you keep a list of who's been paid and who's yet to be paid. If anyone needs to be paid on the day, have that cash ready.

Little extras

Little things like guest books, pens, toiletry baskets and signage often get left until the last minute or forgotten completely. Go into your mind palace and run through the events of your day from the perspective of a guest - it will help you think about anything you might have missed.

Pack your emergency kit

It's always a good idea to bring a little kit of things you might need, just in case. This could be anything from needle and thread (for buttons) to baby wipes and deodorant for nervous sweating.

Break out (in) your dancing shoes

If you and your soon-to-be spouse have new shoes for the big day, DO NOT leave it to the morning of your wedding to spend any time in them. You need to wear them in and scuff the soles up a little so you're not slipping everywhere a la Chandler Bing, or covered in blisters for your honeymoon, painfully hobbling to and from the beach.

Get a haircut

If you just need a trim, you're fine to go a week before – but not any closer. If you need an actual, proper haircut, book it three to four weeks before, or risk facing the all-too-common experience of getting it cut too short at the salon, politely nodding and smiling at the mirror behind your head, then crying silently in the car. Give yourself a few weeks to get used to any new length

Prepare to get away

Oh yeah, that holiday you've got planned as a reward for all your hard work getting married! You'd be surprised how easy it is to forget about prep for your honeymoon as you enter the final weeks of wedding prep. Start packing a bag, order your currency and buy your travel insurance.

Musical numbers

One thing that couples often forget to do (because you have enough going on) is to have a few playlists lined up for background music. Whether it's for the time pre-ceremony as guests take their seats or during dinner, have a few playlists up your sleeve and put someone in charge of cueing them up.

The gift of giving

Order the gifts you'll be giving to your loved ones on the day as thank-you gifts - flowers for mums, hampers for your bridesmaids - and arrange for some of your wedding party to help hand them out in advance.

Try to chill

Now is the time to get some rest and spend some time with that lovely other half of yours before you take this next step. In the chaos of wedding planning it can be easy to lose sight of the end game, which is a new chapter with each other (full of smugness and love). Spend some time together with weddings off the agenda (straight up *ban* the word from your evening) and enjoy your last few weeks as a soon-to-be-marrieds.

HOW TO NOT BE A DICK ON YOUR WEDDING DAY

It's your day – great, we get it. But that doesn't give you an excuse to behave badly.

Feed people

Please feed people, and we don't just mean your guests. Feed your suppliers. If they are there for the majority of the day, they need to eat. They don't need a three-course banquet, but for God's sake give them a meal. This is normally your photographer, videographer, coordinator and the band – don't forget them in the catering count. Their tummies will appreciate it.

Don't look for problems

If the napkins aren't folded exactly as you imagined or if the cake table is on the other side of the room, don't freak out. It doesn't matter. Every wedding has its hiccups, no matter how impeccably planned it is. That's just life.

The small things that you think are a big deal won't be noticed by anybody else so don't worry about them on the day.

Trust your suppliers

You hired them – if you vetted them properly, you know they're good. Let them get on with their job and don't second guess or question them. As long as you've briefed them properly they'll be fine and they'll appreciate not being micro-managed on the day.

Tell people what's going on

At least give your nearest and dearest a heads-up so they know how the day will flow and any particular tasks they have. As for everyone else, a rough over-view of what's happening when with some signage should help. Let's face it, everyone just wants to know where their next meal is coming from - in life, and in weddings.

Enjoy yourself!

Everything you've worked for is finally here and it will be gone in a flash! Relax, try not to get hammered, and appreciate spending the day with everyone you like enough to buy dinner for. They're here for you, enjoy their company.

WHEN THE CONFETTI HAS SETTLED

JU5T M4RR1ED

High freakin' five - you just got hitched! Like, all your hard work just paid off and you (hopefully) had an epic day you won't forget in a hurry.

But for better or worse, the admin doesn't stop after you've unpacked your honeymoon suitcase. There are a few things still to wrap up which you'll be glad you did in the long-run.

Send thank-you notes

Your parents didn't raise an ingrate. Send your guests thank-you notes for their gifts and for spending the day with you.

Thank your suppliers

A lot of wedding suppliers are *super* invested in your day, and sometimes if you've been working together a long time, it's basically like a friend just walked down the aisle, not a client. A little thank you goes a long way.

And if you've had a good experience, say so! The best way you can do that is by leaving a review on Google and sending them a testimonial.

Get your cash back

Don't forget about all that bonus cash you paid up-front just in case you broke something. Assuming you didn't break anything and hide it under a rug, get those deposits back!

Sell or pass on your decor

Because what the hell are you going to do with 1000 tea light holders and a dozen hand-painted terracotta table numbers? Figure out what you're going to keep for posterity and what can be useful in your own home. Donate or sell the rest.

Clean, donate or sell your outfits

Consider professionally cleaning and storing your attire. You might want to save it for your daughter's future wedding, a ten-year anniversary vow renewal, or just for reminiscing's sake.

You can also donate or sell your wedding dress to help out other brides (and, in the process, be kind to the environment).

Buy a keepsake box

All those spare invitations, photo booth prints and dress swatches have got to go somewhere, so buy a dedicated keepsake box for all your wedding memorabilia - you'll want to look at it all again someday.

Take down your wedding website

It's served its purpose and now it's destined for the internet graveyard, along with MySpace and NeoPets.

So unless you want to use it to share embarrassing dance floor pics from the wedding, or start a family-based blog so the world and his wife can follow along with your post-wedding life, maybe take it down.

Change your names (if you want)

Don't leave this ballache admin job too long. If you're changing your names, fill out the paperwork, get all new licences and passports, and have a lovely, clean start without it hanging over your head.

Take on a challenge

Wedding comedown can be tough for some - you've poured most of your emotional energy into throwing a party for a long time (maybe years!) and you might find it difficult to just go cold turkey and like, not have a spreadsheet for something. Give yourself a project, learn a new skill or buy a really hard puzzle.

Revel

Much like you should do at the start of your engagement, so should you at the start of your newly married life. Regardless of whether you've been together for two years or 20, it's still all new – revel in your badass newlywed status.

IN CONCLUSION

If you're reading this and you've got a brand new ring on your finger - BLOODY HELL MATE, CONGRATS! You did it, you survived to tell the tale, and you got a brand new life partner to boot.

If you're still yet to walk down the aisle – you've got this, pal. If this book has made wedding planning even an iota easier, we will die happy planners.

We hope we've been able to show you not only that you are able to plan your own wedding without committing an act of murder, but also that you're able to be more free in your choices. We are massive believers in rulebook-free weddings and fun, personality-filled days, and we hope you can plan the wedding you want to have with the help of this book.

LOVE YOU BYE!

—

Psst! Your password for hacking into our mainframe and getting your mitts on our editable planning templates we referenced throughout is 'unruly21', download these at www.jointherevelry.com/unrulybook

ACKNOWLEDGEMENTS

A massive thank you to every bride and groom we have worked with over the last 13 years, who have trusted us as wedding planners and given us the privilege of gaining the experience we hope comes across in this book.

To every supplier who contributed their pro tips, we thank you from the bottom of our hearts:

Celebrant Nat Raybould - natraybouldweds.com
Caviar & Chips - caviarandchips.co.uk
White Cottage Weddings whitecottageweddings.com
Hair & Makeup Atelier hairandmakeupatelier.com
Whisk & Drizzle whiskanddrizzle.co.uk

To Kelly and Toby at White Cottage who designed our bangin' front cover and graphics - you blow us away.

To our husbands, James and Robbie, who endlessly proof-read and made suggestions for different headings that we consistently ignored. And to our children, Hazel and Willow, Finlay and Max - thank you for being our motivation and our best cheerleaders, and also for giving us a few moments bloody peace every so often to write the damn thing.

ABOUT THE AUTHORS

Unruly was written by Holly Poulter and Susannah Dale, award-winning wedding planners at Revelry Events based in London and Glasgow.

Holly has been in the wedding game for as long as she remembers - being the seven-year-old who planned the fake lunchtime weddings you had in the playground at primary school. She interned throughout her teens and finally started her own venture into planning at just 19.

Susannah spent the first half of her career in PR and events working for big London agencies. She was creating events and campaigns for UK and global brands before realising it just wasn't fulfilling her anymore. She fell in love with Holly's work and asked if she could shadow her for a summer. They clicked, and a partnership was born.

Together, Holly and Susannah have built Revelry into a multi-award-winning planning and design company. Their work has been featured in key wedding titles such as Brides, Your & Your Wedding and Wedding Ideas as well as Grazia, BBC Radio, Vogue, Time Out, The Times, Sky News and Channel 5.

www.jointherevelry.com

FEEDBACK + WIN

We're thrilled you chose to flip through our little book and we'd LOVE to hear what you thought about it.

We also – like you – love winning stuff. So if you'd like to be in with a chance to win a £50 John Lewis voucher to get a head start on that gift list, head over to our quick little Google Form in the link below and tell us what you liked and didn't like (be honest). We'll be holding a prize draw towards the end of the year.

https://forms.gle/ynV3idsnAZY6tjtW9

Printed in Great Britain
by Amazon